All the stuff that I'm not interested in gets saved in the junk file.

When I'm older, I might be a storm chaser.

The only thing I can't hear is the footprints of a bug.

...he'll be able to see my muscles growing in my body.

I'm a bat, and bats see best in the dark.

Through the gift of asking thoughtful questions to learn

and listening, to truly understand, this book was born.

We dedicate our work to the grace we're all given

to do the same for each other.

IF I SQUEEZE YOUR HEAD → I'm sorry.

FOREWORD

Rylan is a brilliant child who is able to provide insightful information into what life is like from his perspective. Any person who is curious about what a child with Tourette's and Autism experiences would benefit from listening to Rylan. I highly recommend this book!

- Chris with Special Books by Special Kids

OUR BIGGEST FANS

"My wife, Dorie, and I were introduced to the extraordinary undertaking of Rylan and his mom, Gwen. This book will enlighten a wide audience of the profound feelings and thoughts of a child with special challenges. We speak from the authority of nearly three decades of experience in the arena of advocating for a child with special needs.

Everyone is challenged, but those that are more challenged have a larger responsibility. Rylan is meeting his. Had Rylan's work been available to us when our son, Christopher, was alive, it would have served as a cornerstone, a reference for perspective, determination and impetus to convince others that despite challenges, we are all God's creations with undeniable abilities.

We love Rylan's work and pray that we may someday give him a hug. We would also be honored to have our heads squeezed."

RICHARD AND DORIE RUSH

Parents of the late Christopher Rush, featured in the film "Go Far"

"This book is a great tool for kids all across the Autism and Tourette's spectrum, as well as their families, friends, teachers and classmates. Knowing that this is written & illustrated from Rylan's perspective, it reminds the reader that Rylan may have Autism and Tourette's, but Autism and Tourette's do not have him. Regardless of a few setbacks, we "Aspies" are as capable as anybody else."

JAMES DURBIN

American Idol Finalist and Lead Singer of "Quiet Riot"

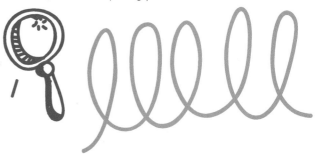

"I'm epically stoked to have the honor of reading this book, which opened my eyes to the wonderful world of Rylan, a remarkably creative child who has gifted the world (along with his equally remarkable mom) with an invaluable resource. As a mom to a child with special needs, I love all of it! Any resource that brings awareness, acceptance, and love is welcome on my book shelf."

JESSICA RONNE

Author and Blogger at "Jess Plus the Mess"

"This book is an amazingly fresh, honest, and authentic perspective of what the world looks like through the eyes of someone with "special" needs. It should be read not only to other special needs children, but to all children and adults to help them better understand that we all have our own unique abilities and disabilities and to not define ourselves based on perceived disabilities."

ZACK ARNOLD

Documentary Director
"GO FAR: The Christopher Rush Story"

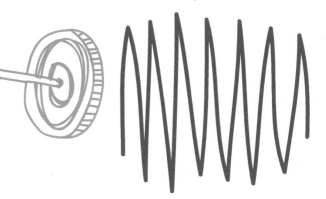

"This book is sheer GENIUS. Rylan owns his diagnosis of Tourette's and Autism with Hulk-like confidence. If "I Squeeze Your Head I'm Sorry", is not only aesthetically delightful, but it helps us all see an inside glimpse at the amazing inter-working of a brain that God blessed with originality, creativity, and sheer brilliance. I can see it boosting the inner-confidence of thousands of readers who need affirmation that uniqueness is awesome.

Vogelzang's book should be on the must-read list of every single teacher and professional who works with children. From an educational standpoint, it provides insight to help inform teaching and it can also serve as a springboard for classroom discussions about special needs and how ALL our brains function in mighty ways. Furthermore, this book will benefit children and youth as a model so that everyone can better articulate how their brains function. This book is a meta-cognitive masterpiece."

SARAH PHILPOTT, PHD

Author & Teacher

"Along with his mom, Rylan has written a dazzling picture book about living with Autism & Tourette Syndrome that is heartwarming enough you'll want to squeeze the book over & over again.

My only complaint? I wish it had come out ten years ago when my own son was diagnosed. Then again, I might have stalked them down & squeezed their heads with gratitude."

ANDREA FRAZER PAVENTI

Author & Tourette's Mama

WHY THIS BOOK?

As my husband and I stood in a Golden, Colorado driveway, Rylan's foster mom handed him to us with eager tears swelling. It was 2007, he was three weeks old, and as I held Rylan to my chest, he was ours.

Just. Like. That.

That instant altered who our family would become. Our son would unveil truths we didn't know to be true, love we had yet to offer, and growth we couldn't have anticipated. It was the beginning of a long journey of patience, joy, advocacy, belly laughing, heartache, and faith. That day we were introduced to a healthy, delicious, egg-shape-headed baby, and I vowed to be his Mama Bird. We've stumbled through twelve years of learning about this complicated human we're raising—our son. He is joy incarnate, even through confusing diagnosis after confusing diagnosis, and we're fierce in our determination to advocate for him and with him. Rylan's labels of Autism and Tourette Syndrome do not define him. But they do influence how we journey as a family.

Through a semester of homeschooling, Rylan created an art show about living with special needs. He drew pictures of what it feels like living inside his brain, many of which explained why he loves to squeeze peoples' heads. It's "one of his things, Broski." Squeezing is one way Rylan releases emotions, namely excitement and stress. If he squeezes your head, he's demonstrating his deep love for you and signaling your inclusion in his inner circle. His impulsivity doesn't give him time to consider how unwelcome the head squeeze may be.

The impact Rylan's art show had on visitors was powerful. It gifted people with the opportunity to see Rylan's heart and tiptoe in his shoes. Two years after the first art show, and through the grace of God, Rylan's art and insightful words have bloomed into the labor of love now resting in your hands. Our work highlights the intricacies of the brain and the awesomely diverse ways in which we associate with the world around us. The subject of inclusion (of all types) has etched itself into our world. The fact that diversity exists is an undeniable gift. Embracing that gift has enriched our path.

Rylan's bravery allows his "beauteous readers" to enter the brain of a child who sees, feels, and understands the world from a remarkable and refreshingly unique perspective. He believes firmly that every human deserves to be heard and understood. He also believes that the dragon series books he's writing will be next to hit shelves near you. Stay tuned, friends. I may be biased as this child's mom, but I'm confident this book will take you on an incredible journey. Deep diving into these pages is an inclusive experience that will uplift, challenge, educate, entertain and create community among the smallest to the tallest humans.

We're "EPICALLY STOKED," as Rylan would say, to walk this journey with you. We appreciate you and your unique brain a bushel and a peck and a squeeze around your neck. Rylan's responsible for the squeeze around the neck part.

The sponge of SQUEEZING

I love to squeeze things that are alive. Of course my dog, my chicken Combuskin, peoples' heads, ya know, your typical squeezing. It's part of what makes me myself. I guess it's why we called the book, "If I Squeeze Your Head I'm Sorry," even though I wanted to make the title "Pokemon are Totally Real Even if Your Mom Says They're Not". When my love comes out, I get so excited and I can't stop my hands from squeezing. Don't get scared; I'm learning to control my squeezing.

I think it's cute to squeeze, but Mom and Dad are not cool with it. Like, ever. Sometimes they grab my hands and arms to stop me from squeezing, and they don't understand that I will keep squeezing until the squeezing gets out of my body.

The robot squeezing the sponge in my drawing represents my hands, because I don't draw hands well. I really like robots, and I will be an inventor of robots when I have a job. When I squeeze, my hands feel like when you close a clothespin and it has to shut. The clothespin can't control when to shut and open, so it's like a robot controlling my hands to squeeze. It's not a tic, but it feels like I can't control my squeezing hands.

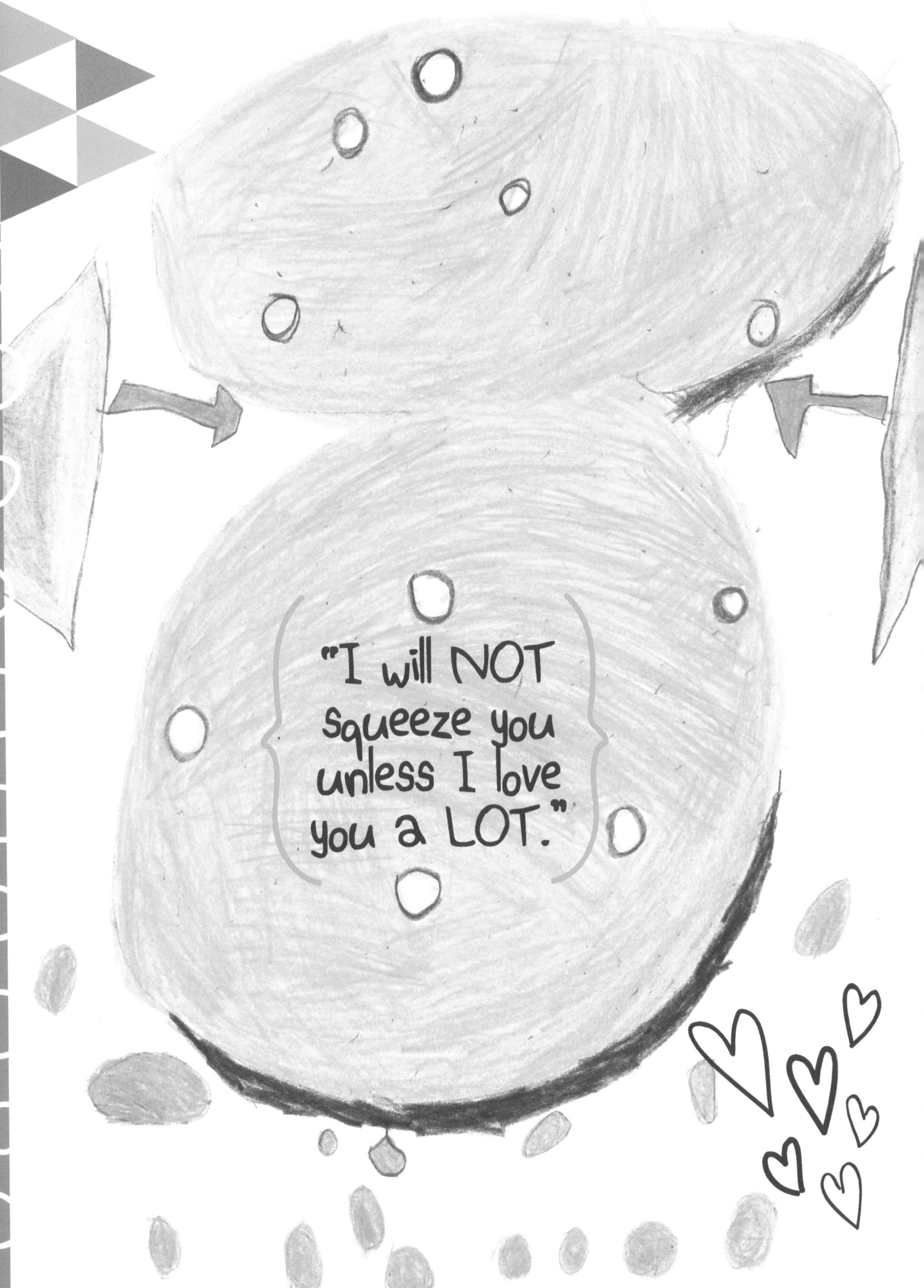
"I will NOT squeeze you unless I love you a LOT."

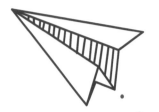

{ "... I see EVERYTHING around me." }

THE MAGNET of the Eye

If there's a distraction, my eyes will find it. There are distractions pretty much everywhere I go, especially at school. My eyes always need exercise and I see EVERYTHING around me. Exercising is not my thing because my pupils and my brain do all the exercising for my day.

When I see something that interests me, I can't look away until something loud in my ear (like a mad dog) tells me to stop. Like my mom saying, "Hey buddy!" Usually she has to say that a lot of times before I snap out of my imagination. Finally, I scare out of my distraction with a jump.

One of my doctors thought I was having seizures because of how often I get distracted, but I'm not. They did lots of tests at the children's hospital to make sure. I even got to sleep at the hospital with my mom and watch TONS of movies. Epic!

When I find something to fix my eyes on, I feel relaxed. But when I'm not fixed on a thing, my eyes always scan for the next interesting thing. It's hard to have this magnet in my eyes because I stare at so many things. The magnet gets me in trouble because I waste time.

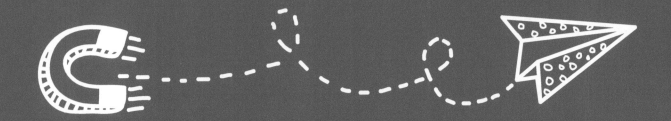

TORNADO
of ideas

When a bunch of ideas come to my brain, I just really have to let them twirl in my head and think about them. I probably get in trouble because I'm thinking about my ideas while other people are doing math or talking to me. I feel mixed up like a tornado.

It's a bad feeling when my head is so full of ideas taking up all the room in my brain, but it also feels good because I have so many interesting thoughts. I forget my ideas because there are so many, and that's why I want to tell people right at the moment I think them. I lose a lot of my ideas. The tornado sucks them up.

I say, "Can I please change the subject?" a lot when I have a thought or question that needs to get out. I confuse people and they say my words are "off topic."

I think tornadoes are epic and scary, and when I'm older I might be a storm chaser so I can follow tornadoes around the land.

"I lose a lot of my ideas. The tornado sucks them up."

"I'm just a regular kid, ya know!"

You might notice my Tourette's, you might not. Depends on the day. A lot of people think I have itchy eyes. Nope, they're not itchy. I just blink a lot. Other people think I'm trying to act like a mouse. Nope! I just like to make squeaking sounds sometimes that are soooo cute. Lots of people ask if my shirt is uncomfortable. Nope! That's just my shoulders shrugging. It's hilarious when people think I'm looking up at Heaven. Nope again! I just need to look at lights a lot—especially the bright-as-the-sun lights at school that make my eyes burn like fire.

Sometimes my tics give me headaches, but mostly they don't hurt me or bother me. I make a lot of noises, and that's hard when I'm at school trying to focus on math. Or when we have a lockdown drill. Hello! I cannot sit in the corner pretending like a bad man is in the hallway and be quiet! My tics go CRAZY when I have to be extra quiet.

I don't notice my tics most of the time, but other people do. They're not contagious, and I don't take any medicine for them. Mom told me the medicine could make me not who I am in my heart, and she doesn't want to change me. I don't have tics when I sleep, but they get worse when I'm super exhausted, or excited, or nervous.

I'm exhausted ALL THE TIME. Having a tic feels like I'm running one MILLION miles. You can ask me about them. It hurts my feelings when people stare at me and whisper or get mad at me for making my tics. I'd rather you ask me to explain. I'm just a regular kid, ya know!

HAND OF

→ pokes

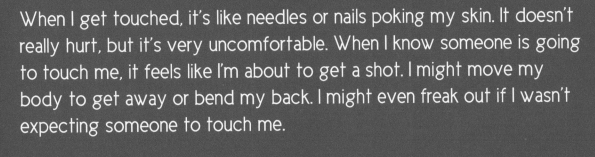

When I get touched, it's like needles or nails poking my skin. It doesn't really hurt, but it's very uncomfortable. When I know someone is going to touch me, it feels like I'm about to get a shot. I might move my body to get away or bend my back. I might even freak out if I wasn't expecting someone to touch me.

I try to say nicely, "Please don't touch me," because I want them to get away, but I don't want to make them mad. It works pretty well. The pokey feeling goes right away after I get touched.

I like it when people ask to give me hugs, because sometimes hugs are okay. And squeezing feels like a soft cloud to me. It's confusing, but I like to touch other people with squeezes or wrestling. My body feels so relaxed after I squeeze. This gets me in trouble because it's not appropriate to squeeze anything that's alive. My dog, Enzo, lets me squeeze him, but Mom and Dad don't like that very much. It just feels sooooo good!

But do NOT squeeze me, please. That does NOT feel good unless I ask you to.

"Birds don't have fears- only joy in their hearts."

So much CONFUSION

That God of mine is super confusing. Sometimes I don't know if He's real. The negative part of my brain tells me there are Greek gods like Zeus, and people in churches worship gods who aren't real. That's confusing to my brain. The positive part of my brain tells me God IS real, because God has helped me a bunch of times in my life. I can barely even think about it because it makes my brain really tired. Maybe God put the confusion into my mind because He doesn't want me to know everything about Him until I go to Heaven.

I think Heaven has a bunch of birds and animals. I would like to be a chickadee when I get there because chickadees are so cute, and because birds can move silently through the sky with no fears in the world. I hope my mom will be a robin so we can be a bird family in Heaven. What would be the point if I'm a bird and my family are people?

Birds don't have fears—only joy in their hearts. Chickens have fear of course, because we eat them. RIGHT, people? I do think angels are real, because when I got hit by a car, an angel lifted me up and saved me.

Dog of LOUDNESS

When I'm in a loud room, the hearing part of my brain is so big that I hear ALL the noise, every sound, like a huge scream. The only thing I can't hear is the footprints of a bug. But if I could, it would sound like a giant stomping on a rug.

Bugs freak me out so much that I start screaming at the sight of a teeny black ant. Once I held an adorable green caterpillar, and I will be so proud of myself for that until I die. But that was enough holding of bugs for me, so don't ask me to hold any more bugs again.

The cafeteria at school and the beginning of summer camps are so loud, they pierce my ear drums like a barking dog. Loud places make me feel like there's a vibrating machine or an earthquake inside my body. I want to get away from those places so my body can feel more calm. I can usually tell the adult in charge when I need to get away because my body talks very loudly to me. A lot of times my adult in charge doesn't understand the dog of loudness, so I have to keep telling them until they let me take a break.

Brain of
SLEEPINESS

This is the brain of sleepiness. It's where my brain gets tired of having to think so much. It gets tired and dizzy, but I don't actually fall asleep because it's SO hard for me to actually fall asleep. Probably an hour every night, I lay in my bed waiting for sleep to dominate my brain. The 1,000-pound blanket Mom bought helps my body to go in to relaxation mode.

My brain only gets sleepy when I have to think about things I'm NOT interested in. This happens a lot at school and when I have to learn boring-to-me things, like math and writing about facts. I actually do hear all the words people say and save them to my junk file, but my body yawns and I want to rest my head on my desk, because the teacher would notice if I put my head on the floor. I just need to make my body comfortable, and that's hard to do at school. I get headaches if I think too hard, because I have so many ideas I need to push aside.

"I have so many ideas I need to push aside."

VIDEO GAME
of Calmness

When I need to feel calm, I want to play video games and play on screens. My brain doesn't have to think much. I can just let my back rest against the couch and push buttons. I literally dream of that magical spot on the couch all day long at school. It's my reward for trying super hard Mom says.

I like any kind of screen, because it's my thing, Broski! I was born to love screens and be a master of technology. I can figure out how things work REALLY well. That's my giftedness, Mom tells me.

Screens don't make my brain too tired. They massage my brain muscles to relax. My parents say screens make my brain work really hard and make me crabby, but I think they relax and squeeze my brain. Do YOU love screens?

CAMPING OUT
with a horse

I'm going to horse camp today. I don't know how I'm going to sleep in a tent with a horse, but whatever. Horses are epic. They make my body feel calm and relaxed. Too bad about all the flies that live with the horses though. I HATE flies. They creep me out. They fly around so fast and annoy me and I don't know what they're going to do.

At breakfast, I saw Mom sprinkle flax into my oat bran and I said, "MOM, no flax seed. I don't want to be farting on the horses." Horses fart a lot, so I don't need to fart too.

Horses have big huge eyes that have so many gleams in them. Mom agrees that I have a lot of gleams in my eyes. I ask her all the time how many I have and if I have over 35 in the morning it will for sure be a good day. One time I had 376 gleams, so it was the best day ever.

Horse Camp
"Horses have big huge eyes that have so many gleams ..."

LIFESAVERS

Save Lives

My little sister is sooo adorable. She is also annoying because she screams and cries and it makes my ears get pokies in them. I just have to cover them with my hands until she's done. I think I scream when she screams because it's so uncomfortable, but I don't know for sure. My brain blocks out all the sound.

Once Reagan was choking on a green bean at dinner, so I started yelling to HURRY and give her a red Life Saver! No one listened to my great idea, but good thing she stopped choking. When she stopped choking, Dad asked me what I was saying and I told him we should stock up on Life Savers with the hole in the middle so we can be safe while choking. I like the red ones best, so that's the flavor I think would help the most. They laughed, but it wasn't funny. Those things save lives!

"They laughed, but it wasn't funny."

Going BATTY

I had to pee SO bad when I woke up at 6:58am this morning. I'm supposed to get out of bed at 7:00am, so I was two minutes too early. Mom isn't mad when I get up too early on school days. (She's the best.)

Dad said, "Dude, please turn on the light so you can aim." I told him that it's not even a problem. I'm a bat, and bats see best in the dark. He smiled so I know he agreed.

Miss Frizzle teaches me about bats, and she wears dresses with bats on them. I LOOOVE Miss Frizzle, and I wish she could be my teacher. I asked my teacher if she could be more like Miss Frizzle and wear bat skirts and be more fun and exciting. And of course get a magic bus that can fly into the human endocrine system. She didn't seem excited when I asked her that, so I will keep asking her until she understands better.

That happens a lot. People don't understand awesome ideas when they get older. Too bad for them.

The SAVE KEY

The save key saves things I need to keep in my mind, but I don't want to use right away. I save writing, reading, math, music, etc. All the stuff that I'm not interested in gets saved in the junk file, and then I'm able to start a whole new file for things I learn next.

Sometimes there's too much in my mind, and it would fill up way too many Google docs, so the Save button helps me to clear my mind. Then I can start a new Google doc.

I have SO many Google docs in my brain. Keeping them organized is impossible, because there are so many. When I can't stay organized with my backpack and my homework and my clothes all over the floor, that's called 'Executive Functioning.' Sounds like a fancy way to say I have an epic brain of imagination.

" ... the Save button helps me to clear my mind."

Wall of DISCOVERY

Mom said this new park we went to would be super fun and not at all scary. We brought Brady with us because I LOVE Brady. His voice is lower than mine so he must be in puberty.

In the car, I asked Mom a lot of questions about this park because I've never been there, and that makes my skin nervous and my brain wants to explode with questions. She didn't know the answers to my questions, so that made my skin even MORE itchy, but she kept telling me that it would be fun.

But what if there's water that comes out of nowhere and freaks me out? What if the inside of the slide is super dark and I get stuck and Mom can't hear me? What if there is lightning and they have loud poles that scream at us like the other park we went to during the thunderstorm?

I chose to sit on the rock wall and watch. Mom checked on me and wanted me to come play, but I chose to watch. After a while, I got excited and jumped up and down, but my skin didn't feel calm yet. The water fountains weren't too crazy and no one cried in them, so I decided it was safe to play in there. Right when I felt calm and ready to investigate the rest of the park with my detective skills, Mom said it was time to go home.

WHAT? That was so unfair.

The Crooked
CABOOSE

In Kindergarten, I was wallking in the middle of the line and Sam touched my arm on purpose. It hurt and was unexpected so I yelled at him and held my arm up high in the air. He told the teacher I was going to hit him. I wasn't. My book at home says hands are not for hitting.

I had to go to the back of the line, and I felt happy because I like to be the caboose. No one can touch you back there, and I can make sounds like a caboose and the teacher doesn't tell me to be quiet in the hall because she's the far-away engine and she can't hear me.

"... I like to be the caboose. No one can touch you back there ..."

Teachers don't understand about being the caboose. They also don't understand that I always make the line crooked because my body likes to move a lot. And I get wobbly walking in a straight line. Basically I like to be a crooked caboose.

BOOM CHICKA LOTTA.

It's loud in the gym, and I cover my ears. It's sharp in my ears when people are so loud. I want to stay in the hall until it's quiet, but my teacher says we all have to go in together. That makes me feel nervous so I cry a little bit and wish my mom was there to take me home.

But I REALLY want to see the dance party in the gym. Sometimes my brain and my body fight about what to do and it's confusing, so I just get nervous and upset. Peoples' words don't really help me feel better, because it just sounds like more noise, and that confuses me.

"... it sounds calm and predictable."

Waves of RELAXATION

I found a painting of waves at therapy. It calmed me. I would just stop in that hallway with unhappy yellow lights in the ceiling and gaze at it. So beautiful.

I wanted to buy it, but Mom kept saying no because I don't have $50. I don't think she knows how beautiful it is, because she didn't look at it for as long as I did. She decided I could color my own waves, so I did. The painting calmed me because it felt like going to the beach and swimming. Waves rush toward the shore and have to relax when they break on the ground. When they hit the shore they stop and the water relaxes and trickles down. Then the water gets hit by another wave and another and another . . .

It also feels like the most coziest rocking chair. It's like I'm in a basket and the sea is carrying me to and fro. The waves are soooo calming and tender. Even when the sea is angry and the waves are like a tyranasaurus rex, my body feels like anything is possible. I could live in the water for my entire life if only my skin didn't turn into one giant prune.

Migrating BUTTERFLIES

I feel like a bunch of butterflies are in my head when I'm trying to think hard. And I mean, a BUNCH. The butterflies try to send messages to my brain, like brainwaves. I have to figure out the problem I'm working on (like math). As I figure things out, the butterflies flutter around. I have to swipe them away, but they keep coming back.

When I'm done thinking, they go back to their home, which is in a different section of my brain. I also have a "Delete" section, a "Gross" section, a "Yeah!" section and a "Like" section. I remember every single detail in all my sections.

I caught a cute caterpillar once when I was five. I was brave enough to touch him. I accidentally squished him, and now he lives in my "Like" section. And in Heaven.

The blue butterflies are God and Jesus, all shiny, and I'm the big red one because I'm different. That's okay with me because it's how God made me.

"The butterflies try to send messages to my brain ..."

"I named him "Blue Puppy" because he's blue and he's a puppy. Duh."

CALMNESS

My tics get real bad when I'm tired and stressed, and I get stressed in the world a lot. Tics are also bad when I'm excited and jumping. I jump when I play video games the most, because my body can't contain my happiness. I have special things that help me feel calm and relaxed, so Mom lets me take them with me when I'm for sure going to be on high alert. My Tourette's does NOT like being on high alert. Watch out!

My cute little bug stuffed animal helped me a lot when I was a little guy. (Boy, was I cute.) My therapist taught me about my bug because he helps kids be brave. He sat on my shoulder wherever I went. No one could see him, but I knew he was there.

When my Gigi was dying I brought Bug to her because she definitely had to be brave before her heart left her body to become a little lamb in Heaven.

Also my blue puppy has been my sidekick since I was four months old. Obviously, I named him "Blue Puppy" because he's blue and he's a puppy. Duh.

TWO JOYS

Probably "Joy" should have been on my birth certificate because everyone tells me that my joy overflows every day in my life. That's not literally true because my joy is not a liquid. But I do have two Joys that live in my headquarters.

What do you think my brain headquarters does when I have a tic? Tics are very important to me, so they have to live in my headquarters. I think there's a monster hiding up there, and sometimes he runs out and puts in his chip, and that makes me have a tic. He's definitely not a friendly emotion. Then I think my anger and sadness join together to form confusion and frustration. That second Joy quickly pushes his chip in so I don't stay frustrated. Good thing I have two Joys up there. It really does help with the tics.

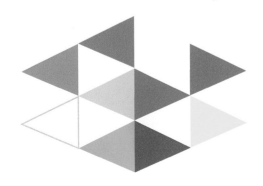

Unpredictable Dark FOREST

Every day my brain is unpredictable. Will it make my speediest powers work? Will it tangle itself in vines, trying to hide from what everyone is telling me to do? Will it be as happy as a tall sunflower? My brain can work by giving me super energy powers or it can be mean to me by making me a dopey slow pokey. I might have too many tics in my brain one day or my brain can make my telekinetic powers shoot water into the clouds, making it rain over my head all day. Sometimes Mom says I wake up on the wrong side of the bed, but that doesn't even make sense. It's my brain that tells me about my day, not my bed.

My classmates are also unpredictable. Will they touch me like vines in the forest? Will they be loud and attack me like a bunch of leopards pouncing out of the trees and landing on me? Some people might be mean like hyenas; they are so mischievous.

My brain is so clogged in the trees I can't even think straight. All these things are unpredictable parts of my life, just like a deep dark forest.

"Will they touch me like vines in the forest?"

HULK

→ kid

A mean kid at school told me that I was weak. That was so rude. I told him that I'm going to start working out under my secret tree at recess with Hunter so he'll be able to see my muscles growing in my body. He laughed, but I wasn't trying to be funny.

People laugh a lot about things that aren't even funny. It happens to me a lot, but when I try to explain that it's not funny they laugh even more. Whatevs.

I saw a picture of a huge muscledude in a magazine one day, and Dad said he must lift lots of weights. That's what I'm going to do. Just wait. I'm gonna be like the Hulk soon. I think the Hulk is epic because obvi, he's super strong and of course he's green and green is my favorite color. One day I put on every pair of pajamas in my drawer all at the same time so I could be like the Hulk and came downstairs to show Papa how massive my muscles were. I was HUGE and he thought it was awesome. Too bad my skin wasn't green. I would have outdid myself. People with green skin would be soooo beautiful, wouldn't they?

"... it is SO joyful to be there."
Stepping stones
=island
=Bush
=river
=Path Of Joy
=Parcore Island
=Base
Meeting place
Land
Island

The PATH OF JOY

If you want to experience the mysterious Path of Joy, from our house in Colorado you walk down the hill to the pool and go to the river behind the pool. Across the stone bridge you'll find a dirt path that is the start of the magic. We named it the Path of Joy because it is SO joyful to be there. It's beautiful, and you can tame fairies there with fairy powder from the magic plants. But you have to do parkour to get to Relaxation Island since it's over the river.

I have fallen in the river, but that's okay when I have on the epic rubber boots that Mom bought for me. There's also Shark Tooth Island and Crawdad Island. The Hyena Fairies try to destroy the King of the Fairies, SoFalla. His wife is SaSpring.

This is the most secret, epic place in the whole entire universe for Cooper, Nate and me. Don't tell everyone you know about it, because it's a private club and only people with special powers are allowed to enter its beauty.

I think every person should have a magic path of joy because everyone can be in nature and we all have joy in our hearts and epic imaginations.

RACE CAR → brain

Sometimes my brain feels like it's racing against my blood cells. It feels really uncomfortable and it hurts my head. I can't think straight, and it takes me off task. I just cannot make it work.

I tell my teachers that I can't think straight because of all the racing. It's really hard to catch up with it. I take breaks to calm down my racing brain. I might eat a piece of candy, talk to a friend, read a book or draw. These breaks help a lot because they end the race with a white flag and finally, the black and white checkered flag. After my break, I can try to focus again as long as my brain keeps a straight path. But I know the twisty, racing path will return..

Hitting the button OF LOVE

♡ ♡ ♡

I have more than 1,000 magic buttons. My favorite is my love button. I think everyone has a love button. Sometimes people do mean things when they forget to push their love button. My love button is ALWAYS pushed.

A boy at Robotics Club called me "Ryan" and that made me so mad because that is not my name. I thought he was being mean and not using his love button. Mom said he wasn't being mean and just didn't know my correct name. I don't think she was right.

Mom's favorite buttons are my cooking and cleaning buttons. She likes it when I push those. But cleaning is super hard for me because my imagination doesn't think about cleaning. (You know—clothes on the floor, legos on my desk, paper all over the place.) I think Mom and Dad should clean all that up for me because God did not make me good at cleaning. My imagination doesn't have time for cleaning.

Mom is a very good cleaner, but it makes her blood boil when there are messes all over the place. I don't know how her blood boils. Volcanos boil, so maybe our blood gets Magma in it like volcanos. I've been thinking about that a lot. I've seen water boil when Dad makes mac n cheese. It bubbles and spits. I don't think our blood should bubble and spit because we would die. Maybe Mom got taught something wrong when she was my age.

"My favorite is my love button."

FINAL THOUGHTS
from Mama Bird

Every human on this beautiful planet was born with one unique brain. We were not created to think, act, believe, or see alike. We were not intended to feel the same feelings or hear the same sounds or understand the same concepts. This world and every intricate thing in it was created with intention and a crazy amount of love. Alongside our complexities, we were gifted with grace. For each other, for our differences, for our similarities, for our brokenness and for our brilliance. Thank you for taking your precious time to enter into Rylan's world. We sure hope that someday he'll have the opportunity to squeeze YOUR head and say sorry for doing so.

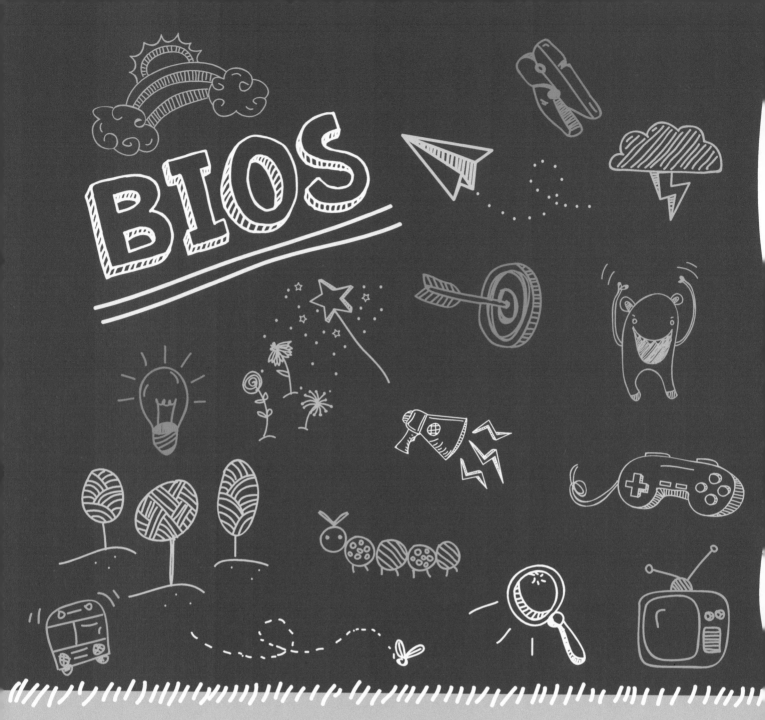

BIOS

Ellie is a freelance graphic designer, entrepeneur and creative spirit. When she isn't designing at her computer, she's burying herself in books, working on her 1978 home nestled among the Colorado pines, or connecting with adoptive and special needs families. She and her husband Stephen work diligently at providing new and creative resources for their daughter Lexi, whose "specialability" of Autism gifts her with refreshing innocence, contagious joy, and an epic brain of imagination. Their younger daughter, Ainsley, has a beautiful heart for encouraging her sister and those around her. Ellie's heart for inclusion and making space for everyone at the table is at the core of her work.

Find out more about Ellie at www.finchandpinedesign.com

Ellie

Gwen is a writer, serial entrepreneur, and gatherer of community. She advocates like a mother for our misunderstood neighbors and adoptive and special needs parents. Gwen left a 15 year career in non-profit marketing to journey through leadership in the world of special needs advocacy and found nothing but grace through the process.

She finds joy in interior design, trees, homemade guacamole, all the books, wine, sarcasm, and podcasts. Gwen owns Four Birds {Airstream Gathering Spaces} and has a lofty list of businesses to launch in the future. She is wife to a handsome Dutchman and mom to Rylan, his independent and kind-spirited younger sister, Reagan, and Mini-Goldendoodle of her dreams, Enzo. They clumsily navigate life in a log cabin in their 5 acre woods in Grand Rapids, Michigan.

Rylan owns his Autism and Tourette Syndrome like a boss. He's an imaginative kid with passion for things that morph, Minecraft, all animals bigger than a Northern Leopard Frog, magic, inventing projects too complicated for his mom and dad to help with, imitating crickets, devouring graphic novels, supportive friends, epic lego sets, telekinesis, God and his adventurous family. He has memorized all 832 Pokemon and their evolutions. and they are alive and well in his daily life. Rylan believes that we all have special needs in our own ways and notices the color of your eyes first. He's epically stoked to become even more famous when his dragon book series gets published.

Join Gwen and Rylan's online community at www.ifisqueezeyourheadimsorry.com and on Instagram @ifisqueezeyourheadimsorry

EPIC
acknowledgements

At the beginning of this grace filled journey was a talented Coloardo cafe owner, Miss Lennon. She challenged us to create an art show and was a champion for Rylan and his work. Through her generosity, we took first steps toward what is now this treasure of a book. Lennon, thank you for seeing him and assuming his tremendous value.

Rylan acknowledges his chickens (Combusken, Jozie, Chickira, and Nugget) for being there when he needs them. They make him feel as calm as a Snorlax Pokemon, they give him exercise when he chases them and they make him giggle uncontrollably, even when they poop all over him. And to his family who makes him feel healthy when he's hungry and joyful when he's blue.

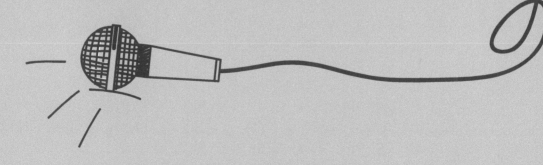

CPSIA information can be obtained
at www.ICGtesting.com
Printed in the USA
LVHW071721271019
635485LV00003B/22/P

* 9 7 8 1 7 3 4 0 7 5 1 2 0 *